SOUL SURVIVOR

Martz

Paperback: 978-1-966652-61-8
eBook: 978-1-966652-62-5
Library of Congress Control Number: 2025902836

Ordering Information:

Prime Seven Media
518 Landmann St.
Tomah City, WI 54660

Printed in the United States of America

Table of Contents

CHAPTER ONE

Testimony

Testimony

I am the one

That can tell you

It's true

We all must believe in God

Hold onto Faith

God is the one

To put you in the right

Place

We go through Pain

Feeling stressed

Lost and confused

But anything is possible

If you just believe

Keep your Faith in him

He can help you

Through Anything Anytime

Pray everyday for every

Blessing you receive

Thanking God

Now i know

He's the only one

I need

Thank you God.

Lost Soul

As youngsters

We don't care

Have no fear

Not really knowing

What's out there

So we live and learn

Everyone gets their turn

To do right or wrong

If you go wrong

You will be a lost soul

Searching for God

To do right You'll live your life

Like you should

Thanking God

Everyday to God we pray

For our blessings

life's a learning lesson

Maybe I was crazy

Never lazy

But God made me understand

That's why now

I'm a righteous man.

Praise To God

Where would I go

What will I see

Who will I be

Looking up to the Sky

Asking God why

You feel so confused

Just look within

God plans everything

Time will tell your story

Coming from him

When you give thanks

It stops the suffering

When you give praise

Your blessed with

Better Days.

Time Is A Healer

With time we all heal

Taught to me by

My Dad he helped

Me understand

My Dad is a wise Man

He taught me to be

A man and he taught me

Work ethics to survive

My life's been a ruff ride

But with time I've healed.

Angel's

When I cry my Angel's

Wipe my tears

They give me love and care

They always care for me

Glad to have my Angel's

With me

You nurses are my Angel's

It's so clear to me

You treat me with respect

You care for me

You provide me what I need

Help me to succeed

To be the best I can be

Without you I'm lost confused

With nothing to lose

You help me understand

Everything I go through

I've got nothing but respect for you

For everything you do.

Confessions

Realize it's true

I can tell you

To hold onto faith in God

When times get hard

You feel pain

Your mind's playing games

Your feeling stressed

Just try your best

God is testing you

To see what your going to do

I know you believe it's True.

7

Higher Power

The only way is up

Nothing can hold me down

I'm too strong

If I fall I stand up tall

I love to brawl

To see who's the fittest

Push my limits to the test

Always working hard

Doing my best not resting

Till it's done

Nothing defeats me

I'm still in this war

I'm hardcore

To the core

Lived my life as an outlaw

Been paid been laid

Stayed in the game

My life changed

When I let God

Take all my stress

Now I just rest

Living my best life.

8

Forever Blesssed

Happiness is our nature

It's my true self

I'm aware

So i only wish for what I want

Do the things I can

I finally realized

I am the man

Who creates his own happiness

Asking mind in no time

You'll have everything

In your dreams.

Religious thoughts

Not everybody is religious

That there is a God

Life teaches you

There is an almighty

Thing's all had to come from

something

It's a mystery God is known

To be the creator of everything

So believing in him

Supposed to bring you everything

You want in this world

So you must have faith

Pray for the thing's to happen

God answers your prayers

All this is possible you are aware.

Blessed Days

All I ever wanted was to be rich

Have what I wanted

I lived a life full of pain

It was lame I was young

Crazy and insane

I done what I had to do

I hung with so many crews

I felt like I had nothing to lose

Now I'm living to be

Happy and free

Living my best life

Being in luxury.

CHAPTER TWO

Learning Lessons

Stay In Lane

Stay In your lane hear what

I'm saying

Things are happening

People ain't playing

With no lives

So many damn lies

Who can say what's real

Or fake anymore

We need to bring back

Love for one another

Care for each other.

Wise Words

People hear but don't understand

It's all part of God's plan for every

Woman and man

To walk there own path

Learn their own mistakes

It takes experience

To be able to admit you went wrong

You hear it in every song life goes on

It don't matter what you got

If you ain't got God.

Mind Stressing

I'm guessing I'm stressed

My heartless breath

Leaves with temptation

With no occupation I'm lost

Searching to find

When I can get mine

Believing in God is all I have

I'm glad he gives me strength

And patience to carry on

My blessings is what God gave me

I live peacefully, God showed me

The path so I proceed to do good

Living my best life like I should.

Depression

I want to be up but

I'm feeling down

Can't find a way out

All I do is thrown

I ain't clowning around

with my pears

All I do is shed tears

Fears of a reality

That ain't really been seen

It's all in my head

All I do is day dream

thinking of situations

Negative vibes so all I do is hide

Can't see a better day

to God I pray

But I'm still feeling depressed

Wanting to take my last

heartless breath.

Pressure

Always on the

go not sure where

Your going to

What you really need to do

Your mind can't process

So many questions

Guessing which one

to choose

You lose focus feeling depressed

You can't rest trying your best

But it ain't good enough

So you break down.

To get your mind right

what you got to do

Is pray to god

He gives you the strength

to carry on.

Suffering

It's all a bad dream

All the thing's your

going through

You don't know what to do

You've got bill's and debts

Debt collectors coming

to collect

You can't pay the debt

Your sitting in your home

All alone no gas or electricity on

So you turn to God and

start to pray

Asking God to give you

Better days and he answers
Your prays and thing's get better
God work's miracles
Just have faith.

17

Time Is A Healer

When thing's get bad

you get sad

My lesson taught to me

by my dad

Is that time is a healer

Thing's always get better

People go through storms

But no matter what your

going through

If you have faith in God

He can help you

through anything

God is good all the time.

Mentally Unstable

Is when people say to you

your unwell

But your unable to process

What they're saying

Your mind is a mess

your lost and confused

All you feel

Is like you've got

nothing to lose

Hoping to stop your mind

racing pacing

Through thoughts

and memories

That you ain't really seen

It's like a bad dream

But your thinking it's real

Mental health is serious

people will kill

We have to understand

Realize it's just a phase

anyone can get

Crazed dazed or lost

We need to stick together

At all costs life is what matters

God is who we need

I hope you understand and succeed

To where you want to be.

Crazy

Going through a manic phase

Is when you turn crazy

Being a menace to society

You need to be in hospital

It's the safest place to be

where you can't

Harm nobody or do

harm to yourself

You mind ain't right

All you feel to do is fight

The right thing to do is accept

the help

Work with people

who can care for you

These are the people

Who can help

you get through

What your going through.

The Breakdown

As you awake you

slowly begin to see

Vision is blurry you are a baby

A small human being

cared for and loved

Incapable of doing for self

All is a mystery

you slowly begin

To process things

Taking everything in

That's happening

using your memory

You begin to lean

Using your emotions

and sensitivities

Your feelings to start to learn

What your going through

As you do you learn to stand

Learn to walk

then you begin to talk

You begin the process of life

As a human being

your raised in a family

Looked after and loved

Going through a process

Of learning as you grow

remembering

The things you learn

understanding

Using feelings emotions

And your sensitivities

We are all one together

living to create

Everything what we see

Manifesting things as you learn

You realize but don't understand

Why thing's happen

the way they do

We are all here to work

But things don't always work out

The way you plan

There are laws

we all have to live by

The laws of physics

The laws of nature

The criminal laws

Everything is put in place

For everyone to learn

understand live by

If we don't we pay the price

The price could be your life

There are punishments

If we break the laws

As you grow

you learn to know

Going through punishments

Experiencing one by one

The things your not

supposed to do

You learn each lesson

but if you don't understand

You continue the same

punishment

So we need to

understand

you get to chose the life

You want to experience

Our true nature

is happiness

To live peacefully

But in this life

it ain't what you see

There is death

wars global warming

Destruction and tragedies

People killing people

You have to look after self

Nobody out there

cares about your

Health, wealth, feeling

love or life

You got to do

what you need to do

This is life you are

the woman or man

That creates your own situations

Experience of life

You are aware

So

within yourself

And always take care.

CHAPTER THREE

Realise

21

Being Aware

Hello mind grant me a wish?

I wish to fly away today

So I believe it

And it come true

When your aware

all you have to do

Is believe for

what you want

And it will manifest

Put it out to the universe

And watch the magic happen

So just believe in yourself

Watch your health,

wealth and love

Grow.

2 2

Lost In Mind

Hi it's me again

your friend mind

Letting you know

everything is fine

Just tell me what you need

And it's guaranteed

I'll grant you your wish

It will come true believe me

you'll see everything

will be okay

So you start to proceed

I wish

I want

I need

Thing's start to manifest

mind your the best

Getting every wish

Things are so great

until you meet hate

And things don't go your way

So you wish

I want

No more

I can't

And your wish

comes true

Because your mind

granted you

What you wished for

Not knowing the laws

of attraction

Until you find him

The awareness within it's you.

2 3

Seeking The Secret

It took me 4 life

times to find

The one thing that mind

or no one tells you

You are you to be happy and free

You are awareness

But your just so unaware

Your minds telling you

To be living in fear

With so much negativity

out there

You ask yourself

Who am I

What am I meant to do

What am i meant to be

Look inside yourself

And tell me it ain't true

That you are aware

And awareness is me

How could this possible be

But consciously

telling yourself differently

And mind makes it come true

So if you already knew why

Would you have to

go through

All the pain going insane

Stuck in this game

there you go again

Stop playing set yourself free

Awaken today be happy

Enjoy an abundance of life

With no limitations

Of what you can achieve

So be aware

But where's aware

Look in the mirror

Right there.

The Beginning

From time I became aware

I started to wish

for all the thing's out there

My visualisations

all came true

I was manifesting everything

i dreamed

And I finally became at peace

The awareness within

Can be like a beast

And a demon within

But have faith in God

and look within Do for self.

25

Self Development

I thank God

For everything I ever had

misunderstanding

Had me wilding as a young man

Now I understand

Why I lived like I did

I never understood things

Growing up as a kid

I had ADHD and Autism

But nobody treated me

I had to live my life

Suffering with mad anxiety

In my teens i turned to weed

To stop my sweaty palms

Walking the streets

s with my blade

I was never afraid of death

God put me through every test

I kept trying my best

I wouldn't rest

Till the work was done

Then I would go out

And start having fun

Being in the night clubs

Partying hard

Getting real drunk

Sleeping all day in my yard

But i wanted better

Then I met my first baby mother

I was Mr lover

So we couldn't be together

I had a son now

I promised to be a better man

I lived a fast life

Years went by then

I had my first daughter

She was my princess

I loved her with all my heart

But her mum kept her away

from me because

I didn't want to be together

Not seeing her drove me crazy

Years went by then I met

Baby mother number 3

I had another daughter

I was so happy

Now I got 3 kids

I spent a lot of time away

Praying one day

I'd be with my kids

But I had a bad gambling habit

It took away everything I had

I had to change

Work on self development

For a better day

So I prayed to god

Started to improve

working on self development

Everyone has to do.

Realization

To be a human being

You will experience

Everything in existence

You will go through all situations

Things that happen good or bad

Life is what you make it

You are wise

Don't be blind to the facts

Live by the laws of attraction

Realize everything

you go through

Your the one

That created the situation

By choosing to

believe your actions

So you go through

the experience

Of life things aren't forever

When you go through an

experience it's just up to you

To learn from the experience

And then choose do you want to

Experience that again

There are no limitations

To what you can experience

No one else can make

choices for you

No one else can go

through your experience

But you you are the one

Who has to live the life

The way you want to live

So live your best life

And be aware.

27

Living

To be living

You are mentally aware

Consciously living to be

Doing the things you desire

Living to work

Living to be free

Living in society of beings

Where anything is possible

There are no limitations

To what you can achieve

Dream believe it's real and it will

Manifest life ain't nothing but a test

Always do your best don't rest

Till it's done that's how

Winning is achieved

Remember to have fun

our true nature

Is to be happy so just be aware.

Power Of Love

Law of attraction

Whatever we imagine

we create

It takes love and belief in self

For thing's to be in reality

Thinking negatively

Will leave you in hard times

Change the balance

of your frequency

By the way you feel

Your life will be amazing

giving love is the best force

Of the law of attraction

It creates whatever we love

It makes things happen

Which you won't believe

All you have to do

Is give love to receive

Life is magnetised

The force is like a boomerang

What we send out

to the universe it

Will return 100 times better

Love is truly all we need.

29

Who Am I

I realized I am aware

The infinite one

life's been a game

Play with no one

Trust nobody do for self

Your the one that cares

About your

Health, Wealth and Happiness

No one can do the things

you want to do for you

You know it's true

so open your eyes and be aware

So there is no more fear

I'm not saying don't care

But show love

Remember not everyone

is your friend

you'll find out in the end

If you don't believe

Just get what you need

Proceed with a good heart

You know right from wrong

Stay within the laws

Of physics

don't ever risk it

And you'll be fine

You must remember

Always believe in yourself

You are the aware.

Control

I really don't know

How long I can hold on

I really don't know

if I can stay strong

My mind can't process

the effects

Without being out of control

I know I'm old

I know I've got

responsibilities

But how the hell can I let it be

This way for me

I said I'm losing my mind

Trying to find a peaceful place

Where can I get rest do my best

Without being arrested

Caught up in the system

I just want to be free

Live happily with sun and sea.

CHAPTER FOUR

Healing

Negative beliefs

Always keep it real

So why do I feel

So much negativity

Is my mind

playing games with me

It all started when

I first heard no

I couldn't believe it

So i fought back slow

Till I got the pain

My brain started hurting

Things weren't the same

My mind told me to be free

Why why are people hating me

No I didn't ask for this

No I don't want no more

But mind grants wishes

So that's what you're asking for

No more pain

But you just asked mind again

So more pain more pain

No I ain't playing the game

So mind does the same

And again came pain

Now all you do is cry

But then you look up in the sky

And ask God why

Mind gives you the answer

And you still say no it wasn't me

But you can't see

That consciously your unaware

That you are the aware.

Recovery

It took me a long time to get my mind right

The battle I had to go through

Learning my illness

Was what me made understand

All the trouble I had

I'm glad I made it through

My manic phases

I give praise to God

For making me wise

I now realize that

I am aware

Of all the situations

And all the experiences

I had to go through

To get where I am I am now

A righteous man

Living in peace working on myself

Being a better man

Life can be great

Once you understand.

God's Grace

You could be in any place

with God's grace

You can make it anywhere

you want to be

God's love for me

Helped me see

Where I was supposed to be

Now I live peacefully

I've got my kid's

With God's grace

I'm going to be a man

I'm going to help my kid's

Understand

To love God.

3 4

Caring For The Carer

Forever being understanding

Of what I'm going through

Nobody really knows

All the thing's you do

To help me see

If I could only be

as good as you

The thing's we do together

Will stay with me forever

Your an angel in my eye's

This one goes out to you

Never would I had made it

wouldn't have kept true

Your the one who made me

a humble guy

I asked God why

But the answer was

in front of my eye's

You were there so plain to see

It's all because

You cared for me.

3 5

The Arrival

This is my story

everything is real

If you don't believe

your going to feel

Every word

It all started when

I first was aware

Born as baby

Unaware of what life

Is out there

But we live and learn

Raised in a society

Endless working days

Racing all the time

Going out of your mind

Till you find God

You might realise the truth

Until you awaken

You will always feel

I am aware.

Life

The one thing you

don't learn in school

Is that life can beat you down

When you go through storms

And there ain't

no one else around

All you have is God

He is the one

who has always been there

But you were so unaware

That God loves you and he cares

God won't walk you too

What he can't walk you through

All you got to do

Is have faith in him

And give him praise

Believe me you will

Have better days.

One Love

All I have is love to give

With much appreciation

For everyone in my life

You stood by me through my hard time's

Gave me a help in hand

You help me learn to live

With my illness

You filled me with love

I'm so grateful to you

For all the thing's you do

Without you

This wouldn't be possible

I want to thank you.

Forever

Happiness is our true nature

It's our true selves

You are aware

So only wish for what you want

Do the thing's you can

You will realise

You are the woman or man

Who creates your own reality

Asking mind in no time

you'll have everything you dream

thing's ain't what they seem

It's all in your mind

Everything is fine

If you truly believe in yourself

All your wealth, health and love

Comes from you

Welcome negativity

Let it be then you'll see

It'll fade away

It's okay the world is fine

Everything is in your mind

You've got nothing to lose

Because consciously

You are aware.

39

Awakening

Going through a spiritual

Awakening

Is the most loneliest thing

You have no one to turn too

All you can do is pray to God

And give thanks' for all you have

When you become awaken

you'll be glad

For everything you been through

I can tell you

Now I am awaken too.

Fresh Start

It's a new beginning for me

I can't be the same no more

I got my mind right

I got work to do

So many thing's to complete

I'm at home with my pen and pad

Writing my rhymes

I want my life to be fine

So I can find

The right woman to

Wine and dine

I'm borderline crazy

Or maybe it was too much stress

Kept away from people

Now I'm living my best life

The struggle people didn't see

It was just God and me

When I was lonely

He never left my side

I give all glory to God

He gave me love

When i had nothing to lose

Now I choose to walk

In righteous shoes

I praise god for giving me

A life I couldn't see

I wonder where I would be

If God didn't choose me

Hear my story

Know all the pain

I've been through

God won't walk you too

What he can't walk

You though I love you God.

The End

Appreciation
And special thanks.

I would like to thank all

my friends and family

Who have always been there

for me throughout

The years of me living

to learn to live with mental health

Bi-polar disorder.

I want to thank my mum and dad

for all the support and love

they have given me

throughout the years

I would like to thank
the mothers of my children
for always doing a great job
taking care of my kids in my absents.
I want to give a special thanks
to all the NHS mental health workers
who have worked and supported me
throughout the years.
I would like to thank you
for reading my poems.

www.ingramcontent.com/pod-product-compliance
Lightning Source LLC
Chambersburg PA
CBHW041121120626
46547CB00019B/2806